Printed in Great Britain
by Amazon

19380995R00119